SUCCESS HABITS FOR TEENS

Powerful Strategies That Help
Teens Be Successful in Life

Jamie Myers

ISBN: 978-1-957590-25-7

For questions, email: Support@AwesomeReads.org

Please consider writing a review!

Just visit: AwesomeReads.org/review

FREE BONUS

SCAN TO GET OUR NEXT BOOK FOR FREE!

TABLE OF CONTENTS

INTRODUCTION

As a teenager, you're entering a new phase in your life, one that is a bridge between childhood and adulthood. While you still have some of the freedom that comes with being a kid, you're also beginning to form the habits that will last a lifetime. It's to your benefit to use this time to develop habits that will lead to success rather than those that aren't as healthy.

This guide will help you establish healthy, productive habits – what we are calling "success habits" – that will carry through to your adult ventures and ensure you're preparing for the life you want to lead. The more consistent you can be in practicing your success habits now, as a teenager, the more likely you will be to carry these habits forward into adulthood, and to reap both their personal and professional benefits.

Opinions differ on how long it takes to create a habit, but you'll need to be committed to exercising on a regular basis for a significant amount of time before it becomes automatic. In fact, studies show that it can take anywhere between 18 and 254 days and an average of 66 days to establish a habit, so if it still feels challenging to you after a few weeks, don't give up. It might just be taking you longer than you expected.

SET GOALS

Setting clear goals and creating a plan to achieve those goals can help people to create the life they want. As such, the first success habit that teenagers should develop is to set goals. When we work toward our goals, we're not only creating a roadmap toward how we want our life to be, but we're also developing positive habits along the way by doing the work it takes to reach each goal.

For example, if you set a goal to improve your grades from Cs to Bs, and make a plan to do so by finishing your homework by 8:00 p.m. each night, you will be developing a habit of getting your homework done early, which is productive and allows you to get a good night's sleep every night. Goals create habits, which is why setting clear goals is the first success habit teenagers should adopt and practice.

SMART GOALS

Now, setting goals isn't as simple as saying, "I have a goal to get all my homework done" and leaving it at that. Goals need to be much more thoughtful and specific than that! It's too easy to abandon general goals that you haven't set up a plan to reach.

For that reason, you need to create SMART goals, which allow you to create a plan to achieve them. SMART stands for specific, measurable, achievable, relevant, and time-bound. These are the characteristics of the types of goals that you are more likely to follow through on and achieve.

Specific

Getting all your homework done might be a noble goal, but it's not specific enough to be consistently achievable. This is because the goal allows some ambiguity or wiggle room: does "all" of your homework mean extra credit, too? What if you complete all of your homework, but you do so after the deadlines for each assignment, so they're all marked late? Technically you've achieved the goal you set, to finish all of your homework, but you haven't done so in a way that is productive or particularly helpful for you. That's because your goal was not specific enough.

When you create a *specific* goal, it needs to be *simple, sensible,* and *significant*. A simple goal is one single thing you want to accomplish. So, for the example of getting all your homework done, you could make it simpler by just identifying homework for a single subject, or a type of homework you have been struggling to complete (i.e. worksheets, essays, etc.). Your new, simpler goal might be, "Finish all of my history homework each night" or "Write every essay the same week it is assigned."

A sensible goal is one that makes sense for what you're trying to accomplish overall. Getting your homework done is a sensible goal because it contributes to longer-term goals like graduating from high school, getting into the college you want, and maybe ultimately even leading the career you want. These long-term ramifications also makes this a significant goal. You need to get your homework done if you want to reach your other long-term goals.

Taking simple, sensible, and significant into account, a specific goal for completing your homework might be, "I will complete all math worksheets assigned as homework each night." This is a simple goal because it only includes one type of homework, but it is also sensible (you need to do your math homework to reach other goals) and significant (not doing your math homework can set you back in school or derail other life goals).

Specific goals always answer the five "W" questions, which are:

- Who: who is involved in this goal?
- What: what is going to be accomplished if the goal is reached?
- When: when will this goal be considered accomplished?
- Where: where will this goal be accomplished?
- Why: why do I want to achieve this goal?

The more specific your goals are, the better you're able to create a plan to reach them and the more satisfied you'll feel when you do.

Measurable

How do you know when you've reached your goal? With a generic goal like getting all of your homework done, you can't. But, if you add in the specificity of getting all math worksheets done every night, you can measure your progress toward that goal because you either completed your math worksheets or you didn't.

Being able to measure progress toward a goal is critical because it allows you to tell whether your plan to achieve the goal is working or not. If it is working and you're making progress, great. If you're not making progress, you can tweak your plan to try another way of reaching your goal. You need to be able to measure your progress along the way toward a goal so that you have time to fix things that aren't working, rather than waiting until too late to realize that you aren't going to meet a goal you've set for yourself.

By making a goal measurable, you're also making it more specific and achievable, which are other characteristics of SMART goals. A goal has to be specific to be measurable and when you create a measurable goal, you can tell whether it's achievable or not. If it's not, you can adjust it until it is.

Achievable

Your goals need to be something you can realistically achieve, otherwise they aren't really goals at all. We all have lofty dreams in mind, but we can't jump ahead to those dream goals right away. Longer-term dreams are achieved by setting up a series of smaller, achievable goals that, one after another, pave the way towards the ultimate dream goal. For instance, you may want to become a veterinarian, but stating that as a goal to achieve right now is not realistic. You have many years of education and training ahead of you and will need to set goals to get through all of that time before you become a veterinarian.

This doesn't mean you should drop your dream goal of becoming a veterinarian just because you can't achieve it yet. It just means you need to set smaller, more achievable goals first. So, maybe you set the goal of earning an A in your sophomore year biology class because you know that a strong understanding of biology will be important to your future training as a veterinarian.

Remember to make sure you can measure your progress toward your goal along the way toward achieving it. If you aren't making progress toward your goal, you may need to reassess whether or not it's actually achievable. For example, if you have a B- average in biology by halfway through the year, that suggests you aren't making good progress towards your goal, and you may want to seek a tutor or talk with your teacher about extra credit work to try to raise your grade and meet the original goal. If those are not possible or aren't helpful for you, then maybe the original goal was not actually achievable – biology can be hard! – and you might want to adjust your goal to a B+ for sophomore biology.

It's important to understand that just because a goal isn't achievable right now doesn't mean it won't ever be. It's okay to modify the sophomore biology goal, knowing you might still ace biology in college. Setting up a series of SMART goals that lead to a larger goal is an effective way to make a long-term dream achievable.

Relevant

Most goals you set are going to be relevant because you wouldn't be setting them otherwise. But you still want to make sure that your goals are worth working on right now or whether other goals might be more relevant at this time in your life. You may have the goal of driving a car, but is that relevant to where you are in life right now? If you don't have a driver's license yet, then the goal of driving a car isn't relevant. Instead, you could set a goal to get your license or permit, which would be more relevant to where you are now, and which are great steps towards that longer-term goal.

When considering the relevance of your goals, think about what you want to achieve now, things that you can't move forward without in the present or near future. These smaller steps will eventually add up to your long-term goals. Right now, you need to focus on goals that will make you successful in what you are doing today.

Time-Bound

Another reason why your goals should be relevant to you now and not sometime in the future is because effective goals are those that are time-bound. When you set a time frame for achieving a goal, you're more likely to stick to it. Without a clear deadline, it's easy to have the same goal for years, or even the rest of our lives, because it never becomes urgent enough to accomplish.

Setting a time limit on your goals helps you prioritize them as well. When you know you have to get something done by a specific time, you'll make that thing a priority. It's especially important not to let everyday tasks get in the way of reaching your goals, so having a deadline can help you set aside time to work toward your goals in increments that will allow you to achieve them before the deadline.

With a clear timeframe to achieve a goal, you can measure your progress and keep track of whether you're on schedule, ahead of schedule, or need to change something in order to meet the deadline. Without an end date, measurements towards a goal are essentially meaningless. You won't be able to determine if you're adequately progressing toward your ultimate goal or if your progress isn't enough to ever reach your goal.

Adding a deadline to your goals gives them urgency and can help to sustain your motivation. It's human nature to do things by the time we say we'll do them, even if we're just promising them to ourselves. We don't want to let ourselves or anyone else down, so we'll work hard to accomplish our goals by the deadlines we've set.

FAILURE

A quick note on failing to reach your goals: this is going to happen. We all sometimes fail to accomplish things we set out to do. The failure itself is not important in the grand scheme of things, even though it often feels very disappointing at the time. What is important is determining the how, why, and where of your failure. Often, the reason we fail can be found in our plans or in the goals themselves – maybe they weren't specific enough, or realistic at a certain time. This is why, as you'll learn in the upcoming section, it is critical to regularly monitor your progress and review your plans toward your goals.

You might have heard the phrase that you learn more from your failures than you do from your successes. This is true, but only if you analyze why you failed so you can start over again with a new goal and a new plan. Whether it's a revision of the goal you failed to meet or a new goal altogether, the important thing is that you keep setting goals for yourself and keep practicing the process of achieving them.

CREATE A PLAN

Reaching your goals requires you to set up a roadmap that will get you to the finish line. Your goals are the finish line, but you can't set up a plan until you know what you're working toward. Using the SMART goals framework will help you establish meaningful, realistic goals. Once you know your goal, you'll set up the roadmap to achieve it.

SMALL INCREMENTS

The best way to achieve goals is to move toward them in small increments. Breaking up a goal into smaller chunks helps you to progress steadily and to celebrate achievements along the way.

One good way to create these small increments is to try backwards planning. Essentially, this means to start at the end goal and work backwards to where you are now, identifying what needs to happen along the way towards the goal. This backward planning strategy can be make planning easier and helps to ensure that you won't forget any steps along the way.

In the image above, you'll see that the ultimate goal for this teen was to submit their essay by October 29. In order to be sure they would meet that goal, they first had to determine the milestones and deadlines that they would need to meet along the way. They planned to meet with their instructor on October 26 to go over their final draft, so they wanted to have their final copy ready for review on October 25.

In order to do that, they knew they would have to spend time editing the draft and estimated that editing would take five days. This meant the student would need to start editing their draft on October 20 in order to have it ready for review by October 25th. Naturally, before editing, they had to have time to actually write that draft. They set October 15th as the day they would start writing the draft and gave themselves five days to finish writing it.

Of course, you can't draft an essay without research. This student wanted to spend some time doing the basic research, and follow that with time organizing the research, to get it ready to begin drafting the essay. They chose to give themselves three days to organize their research and three days before that to do the research. Prior to starting research, they needed to determine the topic of their essay, which was essentially the first step they had to take to get to the end goal of submitting their essay.

Depending on how much support you need to get to your goal, you should add as many smaller increments as necessary. For example, this student only needed the larger steps of researching, organizing, writing, editing, reviewing, meeting with the instructor, and submitting the essay. Some students might need additional steps such as having the introductory paragraph done on October 15, having two body paragraphs done on October 16, having four body paragraphs done on October 17, having the conclusion done on October 18, and so on.

Your plan does not have to be the same as anyone else's plan because your processes are not the same as anyone else's. You might need 10 small steps to accomplish your goal while someone else only needs five. That's fine. In fact, the smaller steps allow you to measure and celebrate your progress more often!

MAKE GOALS VISIBLE

Setting goals in your head is a good start, but if you're really serious about achieving them, you'll need to write them down. Making your goals visible in some way makes them more concrete, which then gives you the motivation to achieve them. Place your written goals in a place where you will see them often. This helps to remind you of your goals and why you set them. Keeping your goals in the forefront of your mind encourages you to take the necessary steps in your plan to achieve them.

You can write down your goals anywhere, but you'll want to test out the location that is most effective for you. Some people use a written planner or organizer to write down their goals. Some organizers are even designed specifically for goal planning. As long as you visit your planner or organizer regularly so you can see your written goals, this is a good strategy.

Other people use a weekly or monthly calendar so they can visualize how much time they have left before the deadlines for their goals. As you see the time between your start and finish dates shrink, you may feel more motivated to complete the steps on your plan. Even if you don't use a wall calendar, you can set up reminders on your phone calendar to keep your goals in front of you.

Sticky notes that are placed in areas you frequent can also be an effective way to remind yourself of your goals. You might put a sticky note of the next day's step on your bathroom mirror so you're reminded of it the first thing in the morning. You can then plan your day to include what needs to get done to accomplish that step. Placing sticky notes on your computer screen, the refrigerator, the door you use to leave your house, and even on the steering wheel of your car will help you to remember your next steps and stay motivated.

There are also various apps that teens can use to plan and track progress towards their goals. These might be convenient if you're already used to checking your phone frequently. Apps that are highly recommended for goal-oriented teens include:

- Teen SMART Goals
- Goals on Track
- Toodledo
- Coach.me

All but one of these apps can help to track habits and goals for free, and you can pay for additional features such as personal coaching, courses, ebooks, and webinars. Goals on Track only offers a free trial and then charges for use of all apps and content, so make sure you have permission from a parent or guardian before signing up for that one.

MONITOR AND CELEBRATE YOUR PROGRESS

Once you start working through the small steps towards your goals, you'll need to frequently check in on your progress. This will allow you to visually check off each step as you complete it, which boosts motivation and can help keep you on track towards your goals. Whether you're using a checklist on your calendar or in your planner, sticky notes, or an app, you'll want to physically indicate that you've completed a mini goal on your way to your larger one. In fact, seeing a step checked off can boost dopamine levels in your brain, which creates a feeling of pleasure and satisfaction. You can look forward to this good feeling each time you accomplish a step towards your goals.

You may want to plan a small reward for yourself as you accomplish each small step towards your goals. For example, you can reward yourself with some time playing a video game you enjoy, or by grabbing a special treat that you reserve just for these occasions.

We don't need a big celebration to satisfy our brain. We just need to give ourselves permission to acknowledge our progress toward our goal. Sometimes, just checking the task off our list is enough of a celebration, but if it isn't, come up with something that will keep you motivated to achieve the next step.

REVIEW YOUR PLAN

When you've reached your goals, your work isn't quite done yet. Take some time to review the plan that got you to the finish line. Looking back over your plan, and all the small things you achieved along the way to your goal, will give you a great sense of accomplishment and a reminder that goal-setting really works.

As you review the plan you've accomplished, note any changes you made along the way. Chances are, you had to tweak your plan every now and then to keep yourself on track. Or, maybe you had to move your deadline back in order to keep the goal achievable. There is nothing wrong with changing a deadline if you realize the first one was unrealistic, as long as you don't make a habit of doing so. Take this opportunity to examine the challenges you faced on your way to meeting your goal and what you did to overcome them. Ask yourself if there was anything you could have done in the planning stage to better prepare for those challenges. Use each plan as a learning opportunity so that the next time around, you can be even more effective at setting SMART goals with realistic timelines.

The accomplishment of one goal can provide great motivation to set a new one and there's no time like the present. Consider what the next logical goal would be that's related to the one you just crossed off your list. You probably already have lots of small goals in mind that will set you on the path to your long-term aspirations. By looking at the entire picture, you'll be able to see that your SMART goals are really just steps toward your really big life goals.

BEGIN WITH THE END IN MIND

The backwards planning technique that you can use for short-term goals such as finishing an essay, doing home-work, or getting a certain grade in a class is also an effective strategy for long-term goals. Whether you want to go to a certain college, have a specific career, retire at a set age, or reach any milestone in your life, you should begin with the end in mind and work your way backward, creating the steps that will take you where you want to go. Very long-term goals will be broken down into steps that are mid- or short-term goals, each of which is broken down into its own mini steps, as described above.

If you try to set big long-term goals without breaking them down into more manageable chunks, you'll have a much harder time achieving them. Remember, many of your long-term goals won't even be achievable or relevant right now, but that's okay. They will become achievable as you complete each of the necessary smaller steps along the way.

Take a look at the various long-term goals in the image above. When you determine what your longest-term goal is (in this case, what an ultimate job title might be), you can work backward from that goal to determine the large steps you have to meet in order to get there. In this case, each title is a large step or a long-term goal. Between those large steps, you'll identify the smaller steps that will get you to each one.

This may sound like a lot of really complicated planning towards very long-term goals like your ideal job title, but don't worry. You can't create a plan or roadmap for each large step yet. It's not feasible to know what steps will take you from being a manager to being a director at this time in your life, and even if you did know, it's likely those steps will change by the time you actually become a manager.

Right now, your focus should be on your first necessary step towards any long-term goal: earning a high school diploma. Create a plan that is made up of the steps you need to take to get your high school diploma. You may need to set even smaller goals before that, for example if you haven't been on the path to reach that goal until now or if you're just now starting to set some goals in your life, and that's perfectly fine. Setting small, realistic steps that you can take now is always a great place to start.

Your desired career path may not appear in the image above. There are many more career paths and job titles out there than one image could ever capture. Furthermore, all of the paths shown in the image require a college degree, but there are many career options that don't. If you're planning to work right out of high school or want to attend a trade school, create a plan for those goals. Regardless of your life plan, the process of identifying and planning towards goals is exactly the same.

By going through an intentional planning process, you're learning how to set yourself up for success, whatever that looks like for you. Don't worry about whether your goals sound as important as someone else's. As long as they're important to you and will keep you motivated toward the life you want to have either now or in the future, they're goals that matter.

PRIORITIZE

Prioritization is a skill that will serve you well no matter what you choose to do in life. The act of prioritizing is choosing which tasks need to be done first before you can move onto others. When you set a goal, you're making your achievement of that goal a priority in your life. Activities that propel you toward your goal become more important than those that don't. This doesn't mean that every goal you set has to be your top priority in life at the time, but articulating a meaningful goal and creating a plan for it is a great way of ensuring it will remain a priority.

Understanding how to prioritize your own activities alongside those that are assigned to you, maybe in school or for a job, is an important skill that will serve you well throughout your life. People who struggle with prioritizing may focus too much time and effort on tasks that should be low priority, neglecting those that are actually more important.

For example, let's take a look at English class assignments for a high school freshman. At the beginning of the year, the student was assigned a capstone project that involves reading a challenging novel and creating a website to market it. The student was required to include specific web pages on the website, and they also had the option to create additional pages for extra credit. The capstone project would be worth 10% of the student's total grade.

Three times throughout the semester, the student was assigned an explanatory essay that they had to write on a topic they want to teach to others. The teacher gave one week to complete each essay, at intervals spread throughout the semester. Altogether, the three essays would be worth 45% of the grade for the class. The student did not have confidence in their writing skills and did not enjoy writing, so they already knew they would have to spend a lot of time on essays to get the grade they want.

Every day throughout the semester, the student had to complete two chapters of assigned reading, and then have to fill out an online questionnaire consisting of five questions about those two chapters. These readings and questionnaires would be worth 20% of the student's grade over the semester.

The remaining 25% of the student's grade would come from participation, other in-class assignments, and exams. Since the teacher dictated when these components of the class would occur, the student didn't have to prioritize them all at the same time.

The student loved technology and, from the first day of class, felt excited about the capstone project. Over the course of the semester, they spent all their time working on it instead of the daily reading or the essays. The consequences of these decisions were that the student got an A on the capstone but only a C on each of the essays, which the student rushed to get done the night before they were due.

What's even worse is that they earned a D on the daily reading and questionnaire tasks. The student hadn't prioritized those throughout the semester. There were so many of those assignments that the student didn't feel concerned about missing a few, and they wanted to really focus on the last project since it seemed so important. After all, it was the capstone.

The overall result is that, despite working very hard on the capstone assignment, the student does not earn the overall grade they had hoped for because they didn't understand how to prioritize their assignments. They chose to work on the task that was most interesting to them instead of the task they don't enjoy (writing), and they also de-prioritized the small daily tasks that actually added up to a significant portion of their overall grade.

This scenario might seem obvious to you, but when you're deciding what tasks to take on first, you would be surprised at how often we procrastinate on the things we *should* do in favor of the things we *want* to do. It's only natural to want to do activities that are pleasurable instead of those that are challenging or unenjoyable. But, in many cases, you have to put difficult and less enjoyable tasks ahead of what you really want to do because they're more important.

So, how do you determine which tasks are more important and therefore a priority? Let's take a look.

THE DIFFERENCE BETWEEN IMPORTANCE AND URGENCY

Before you can start to prioritize the activities in your life, you have to understand the difference between importance and urgency. Most things you do in your everyday life are important, at least to you. Few things are urgent, but those that are urgent need to be prioritized.

Typically, urgent activities have an imminent deadline. These are tasks that must be done to avoid a certain negative outcome. In thinking about the scenario presented in the introduction of this section, the student has three assignments that have specific deadlines, but one of those deadlines is much sooner than the other two. The one with the closest deadline is the urgent task and should be prioritized first. It also happens to have the most impact on the student's grade, thus intensifying its urgency.

Urgent tasks don't have to be the most time consuming (that would probably be the capstone project in our example) and they don't have to have a significant impact on your life (you probably don't need to remember every single fact from the questionnaires you complete). You might think these activities are trivial, but you still have to prioritize them because you have the shortest window in which to accomplish them.

On the other hand, important tasks are those that may be meaningful to you but don't have an immediate deadline. In the earlier scenario, the capstone project is important to the student because they love technology, they want to learn website design skills, and because they know it's the final project for the class. But its deadline is much further in the future. So the student can work on that project when they have time and when there is nothing more pressing that needs attention first. At the early part of the semester, there are other assignments that are more urgent than the capstone.

Consequences often play a part in determining the urgency of a task. For instance, if you have to decide between doing an unwelcome chore at home, with the consequence that you'll lose your phone if you don't do it, and writing a thank you note to your grandma for your birthday gift, which has no immediate consequences if you don't do it, you're probably going to choose to do the chore first.

Now, if that letter to your grandma is put off long enough, there probably will be consequences attached to that delay. Maybe you won't get a birthday gift from her next year if you don't write one. At that point, your letter becomes urgent and will take priority over another task with a lesser consequence.

Of course, this is a simplistic example with clearly defined consequences to show you the difference between urgent and importance. Sometimes, the consequences aren't quite as clear or several tasks appear to have the same urgency and consequences. How do you prioritize them to set yourself up for success?

IDENTIFYING THE MOST URGENT ACTIVITIES

As mentioned above, the consequences of an activity usually help to determine its urgency. No matter how old you are or what you're doing in life, you will always have consequences for not completing tasks that are your responsibility. You have to decide whether those consequences make an activity urgent or not. Many adults must constantly determine whether a particular work activity is more important than a particular family activity. These decisions can be difficult as the stakes get higher, so it's good to practice prioritizing now and make it into a strong habit.

Right now, you might not be dealing with life-changing consequences such as losing a job, but you still face situations that might have negative consequences. For example, you

30

might get a poor grade or not be allowed to go on a field trip if you don't do your homework. You could have to do extra chores at home if you don't do the ones you're already assigned. That trip you're planning for spring break? It might not happen if you bring home a report card with Ds and Fs.

Of course, consequences aren't the only way to determine a task's urgency, and if multiple activities are associated with the same consequences, you'll need to use another metric to determine which one to complete first. Due dates and deadlines are often the tiebreaker between two or more activities that have similar consequences for not completing them on time.

Think about several homework assignments you may have. They all have the same consequences because they're all tied to your grades. But they probably don't all have the same due dates. You are doing yourself a disservice if you choose to complete tasks that have a later deadline before those that have an earlier deadline. Ultimately, you'll find yourself tight on time and probably face some negative consequences as the earlier deadlines approach – losing sleep, feeling unnecessary stress, or earning a lower grade.

Prioritizing your tasks by deadline will allow you to plan ahead to meet your deadlines and avoid any consequences tied to missing them. Just as you can create a plan to meet goals as described in the first section, you should also create a plan to accomplish your tasks by their deadlines. Work backward from the due date to create mini-milestones you need to meet to reach the final deadline.

DAILY CHECKLIST

Just like for your goals, you should write your tasks down in a planner, on a calendar, or in an app so they stay in front of you throughout your day. It can be easy to get busy, forget the things you have to do, and then panic sets in when you run out of time to get them done. We recommend creating a daily checklist that you where cross things off when you complete them and add new tasks to as they arise. For the sake of efficiency and organization, include personal, work, and school items all on the same to-do list rather than having multiple separate lists to keep track of.

Every morning, write the list of everything you have to do for the day, from the routine (doing homework or going to basketball practice) to the out-of-ordinary (submitting an application for summer camp or meeting with your teacher for extra help). Once you have everything in front of you on the list, prioritize the items by their due dates and consequences.

Some things may stay on your list for several days (or weeks) depending on how urgent they are in relation to other tasks. This is perfectly okay. Eventually, those tasks will move up in urgency as their deadlines approach.

Try to stick to your priorities throughout the day and resist the temptation to complete less urgent tasks before others that take priority. Remember that your goal is to get those urgent tasks done and out of the way so that you don't have to scramble when their deadlines approach.

ASK FOR GUIDANCE

Sometimes it's difficult to know which activities to prioritize, especially when you're overwhelmed with many at one time. When this happens, and it will, know that you're not alone and there are people around you who can help you prioritize your tasks. Your parents, teachers, and other trusted adults can give you guidance and insight into your to-do list.

As with many things in your life, your parents or guardians are probably the first people to go to when you're stuck. They have been prioritizing things all their lives and can help you sort through your tasks to get to the heart of what is most urgent on your list. They can help you organize your activities by due date or talk through the potential consequences associated with specific items. Getting insight into some of those consequences from a trusted adult can help you to better prioritize them.

In school, when you have six or seven classes and each teacher has to make sure you understand their material, there are bound to be big deadlines that land on the same day. This can make it hard for you to prioritize your assignments, alongside everything else on your plate. If you're struggling to get started on assignments that are due at the same time and that have the same consequences, talk to your teachers. They can help you plan out your approach toward completing these assignments. They might even be able to change a deadline or provide an extension, especially if several students are in the same situation.

Part of a teacher's job at the high school level is to teach you how to organize your work and create a plan to complete it on time. They are more than willing to give you strategies for handling multiple assignments with close deadlines. Be proactive and ask for help well before the due date so your teacher has enough time to assist you with prioritizing your tasks and creating a plan to get your work done on time.

If you have a part-time job, you will need to prioritize your job tasks while you are on the clock. Your boss will expect you to do the work you're being paid for and not other activities during work hours, such as school work or personal projects. You will need to know how to prioritize the tasks you are given at work so that you complete them by the time your shift is over.

At your age and experience level, your boss will usually tell you what tasks you should complete first during your shift. For example, if you work at a fast food restaurant, helping customers order their food might be your number one priority. If there are no customers in the restaurant, your boss will likely tell you what you should do and in what order. They might tell you to stock supplies first, then wipe down the counters, and then sweep the floors last.

If you're ever in doubt about what task should take priority after your main job duties, ask your boss so you can be sure you don't miss something that should have been at the top of your list. Most bosses would rather you ask about priorities rather than trying to figure them out yourself if they're unclear. Remember that you're all working toward the same goals at a job, so your boss will want everyone to know their priorities so you all can succeed together.

Be aware that there will come a time, probably more than once, when you get conflicting advice over what should be prioritized on your list. Who do you listen to? The best way to handle this is to consider the consequences for not completing each action. Unless the consequences are identical, you'll be able to determine which consequences will be worse if you don't get something done on time.

You can also use your trusted adults for advice about competing priorities. Your parents, for example, are probably the primary people you should listen to at this stage in your life. You can tell them what your teachers or boss said and they can help you formulate a plan.

Communication is really the key to successfully dealing with conflicting priorities. People are generally understanding if you approach them with your dilemma well before a deadline approaches. This gives you and them enough time to develop a plan to make sure everything gets done on time. Sometimes deadlines are flexible, which can eliminate the conflict. When they're not flexible, though, just letting everyone involved know that there is a conflict can go a long way in making sure the consequences aren't as severe.

Another way to break a priority tie is to look at which task you can get out of the way the quickest. If there's one task that is a high priority but will not take you long to do, place that ahead of the task that will take more time. That way, you can cross one of the items off your list and dedicate the rest of your focus on the other activity that's going to take longer.

Prioritization is a critical life skill. It will allow you to get everything done on time and give you insight into when you might be taking on more than you can handle. Once you get the hang of prioritizing tasks, you'll probably see that you have more time in your day for things you want to do because you're no longer procrastinating about things you have to get done.

BE PROACTIVE

Learning how to ask for what you need to be successful and to take control of your own outcomes is the next success habit for teens that we'll be discussing. This is not an easy habit because we all want to be able to succeed on our own. But sometimes, we don't have all the tools we need or we might not even know what we need to move forward with a project or goal. This section is about knowing when to advocate for your needs and learning strategies for getting those needs met.

WHAT DO YOU NEED TO BE SUCCESSFUL

Whether you're tackling a project in school or searching for a job after you graduate, you're going to need outside resources to help you achieve your goal. Part of planning ahead to ensure your success is knowing what you need to get you to the finish line. You may need more tools (e.g., a computer, access to the internet, or books), education, practice, or other people to assist you along the way. But until you ask for these things, no one is going to know you need them.

When you're creating your plan on how to complete a task (setting goals and establishing priorities), you should consider what you're going to need for each step along the way. This should be a part of your overall plan so you are able to seek the tools, education, practice, or other people you'll need to be successful. Let's take a look at an example.

Your social studies teacher has assigned a project that's due in three weeks. It involves researching a topic, creating a PowerPoint that you will present in front of the class, and interviewing an expert on the topic. When you begin to make your plan, you realize you don't know where to find an expert on the topic you've selected. You also are a little afraid of public speaking and are worried about the presentation component of the project.

As you work backward from the due date, you set several mini-goals along the way that you'll need to meet. These might include select a topic, begin research, schedule interview, complete interview, finish research, organize research, begin presentation draft, finish presentation draft, edit presentation draft, finish presentation, practice giving presentation, submit presentation, and give presentation.

For each step along the way, think about the tools you'll need to complete that step. Generally, your teacher will have provided you with the education and major tools you'll need to complete this project, such as lessons on the topic and access to books and other resources for research. You will have a tool that allows you to create a presentation and you'll probably have been instructed on how to use that tool.

Individually, though, you may be lacking some things you'll need to be successful. For instance, you don't know where to find an expert on your topic. That's a missing piece you're going to need in order to finish move past the third mini-goal in your plan. Well before your deadline for that third mini-goal arrives, you need to get the information you need to schedule that interview.

Since some students are already comfortable with presenting in front of a class, the teacher only provides a short amount of time in class to practice. But you're nervous about giving your presentation, so you may need extra practice time before you get to the day of the actual presentation.

When you finish making your roadmap to the end goal, you should have a list of things you still need in order to complete the project. In this case, you need to know where to find an expert on your topic and you need additional practice time for your presentation. The next part of the process is to find out how you can meet those needs.

WHO CAN HELP YOU GET WHAT YOU NEED?

While you can often find the tools, education, and other resources you need to be successful yourself, there are times when you'll have to pull in other people to help you find what you need. It's a good idea to have a list of people you can rely on to assist you in these situations. Your parents, teachers, coaches, counselors, and friends are all good resources to have around you when you find yourself unable to move forward toward a goal or the completion of a task.

In the case above, to find an expert to interview for your project, you may want to reach out to someone who has connections to experts in your topic or who can at least point you in the right direction. Your social studies teacher would likely be the first person you would talk to in this situation.

We know that your topic is related to social studies and your teacher likely has a network of people you can contact for an interview. If your teacher doesn't have a direct contact, they may be able to give you ideas of where you can find what you need.

For example, if your topic is on your state's history, your teacher may suggest that you start your quest for an expert to interview at a state history museum. You would then contact the museum and ask if they have someone who would be willing to be interviewed for a school project.

Most likely, in this scenario, contacting the museum would provide you with what you need for your interview, but if it didn't, you would continue seeking assistance from various people until you find it. If the museum didn't have an expert who would give an interview, they would probably be able to get you additional contacts to try. Each person you talk to will get you closer to finding what you need.

Getting the interview with an expert will fill the first hole in the roadmap leading to the project's completion. From there, you can almost finish the entire presentation before you run into your next roadblock. The second hole in your plan is getting additional practice time for you to feel comfortable giving your presentation in front of your class. You'll have to reach out to other people in your sphere to help you with this one as well.

Your parents and friends can act as live audiences for additional presentation practices outside of school. Be sure to plan your practice sessions in advance, so that friends and family can put them into their schedules. This means you should have designated practice days built into your roadmap and be prepared to talk to your friends and family members as early as possible.

You might also ask your teacher about additional practice time in school if you're still feeling uncomfortable about giving your presentation. Teachers and counselors might also give you leads for additional educational opportunities that can teach you more about public speaking. These opportunities can boost your confidence, help you build strong public speaking skills, and allow you even more practice time to prepare you for your presentation.

As you get older, you will increase the network of people who can help you get what you need to meet your goals. At times, the people themselves will be the resources you need to finish a task and you'll be able to delegate some of your work to them. This is not always appropriate in a school context, where projects are designed to assess what you've learned as an individual, but as you move into the workforce, delegation can be a powerful tool for getting things done.

TURN FAILURES INTO OPPORTUNITIES

It's frustrating and upsetting when you don't meet your goals or finish a project on time. But after you get over the initial disappointment, you can learn from your failure. This won't be the first time that you'll face a challenging situation, and you'll see that challenging situations are often just repetitions of similar situations you've faced before. This means that you can reflect on a failure and know how to do better the next time.

Turning failures into learning opportunities is a proactive approach to future endeavors. This is done by looking at why you may have failed at a certain goal, and putting a plan in place for the next time you face a similar situation. That similar situation may occur right away or it might be years in the future, but your brain will recall the lessons you learned when something didn't go the way you had hoped it would.

To begin the reflection process, think first about what went wrong. Pinpoint the areas that led to the failure. Perhaps you didn't plan far enough in advance and so you didn't have time to complete all the steps necessary to reach your goal. Maybe you prioritized the wrong tasks and weren't able to complete the more important activities that were critical to success. Whatever it is that prevented you from achieving your goal, take note of it.

Next, ask yourself how you could improve on those areas that weren't successful next time. This is a key part of reflection even if you did achieve your goal because there are always places where we can get stronger in our processes to better our outcomes. Write down the improvements you think of so you can recall them later when you need them. For example, if you identified that you didn't start planning early enough, one of your improvements will be to start your plan as soon as you know about the task or activity instead of waiting a few days or weeks to get started.

Sometimes, a lack of resources can lead to failure and maybe you didn't know what you needed until it was too late. When reflecting on your failure, try to determine if there were tools, education, practice, or other resources that could have made a difference in the outcome. In this case, maybe you needed help with prioritizing individual tasks since they all seemed to have the same consequences and deadlines. Who could you have asked to help you prioritize those activities? If you face a similar situation again, what tools do you now know you'll need to have in place?

The more you think about what went wrong in this instance that you could have changed or handled differently, the better prepared you'll be in similar situations in the future. Don't be afraid to seek others' advice about what you could do to change the outcome next time. Teachers, guardians, and friends are there to guide you as you develop your life skills.

CHALLENGE NEGATIVE THINKING

When trying to be proactive, it can be easy to talk yourself out of asking for what you need by thinking about all the possible negative outcomes. You might think the answer is automatically going to be "no," so why bother? But the truth is, you don't really know what the answer is going to be unless you ask. Fear of rejection often prevents us from getting what we need and as a result, we aren't as successful as we could be.

Of course, no one wants to feel rejected, especially if they believe that getting what they need is the key to overcoming a challenge. But rejection is something we all have to learn how to deal with and the best way to do that is to realize that rejection isn't as scary as it seems. It isn't the end of the world and it might not even be a negative outcome. If rejection leads you down another path that turns out to be an even better solution than your original request, you'll be thankful for that initial "no."

To start taking the fear out of rejection, you'll want to imagine the worst that could happen if you don't get what you need. In our earlier scenario about needing an expert to interview for a project, what would happen if the interview did not go well or as expected? To determine the consequences for tanking that part out of your presentation, you would have to look at the rubric for the assignment or ask your teacher. Let's say that if everything goes wrong with the interview, the highest grade you can get on the project is a B.

Now, the first thing is to reassure yourself. Even if this project receives a B, even if everything goes wrong with the interview, that is not enough to bring your overall grade for the course down.

Another worst-case scenario is that you would change your topic to one for which you know you can get an expert to interview. This might cause a time crunch, but it could be better than getting a lower grade than you want, particularly if it's going to affect your grade point average.

The point of thinking about the worst things that could happen if you can't get what you need is to show you that you have options. They might not be the best options, but a "no" isn't the end of the world. In fact, it could be the beginning of something even better.

Another way to overcome fear of rejection is to connect with why you are there and doing these things in the first place. The point of these assignments is not to receive an A. The A is just a symbol representing that you learned what you needed to learn from the class. Connect with why the interview is important — it is practice for things you are most likely going to have to do on a larger scale later on. That's it — practice. If you don't practice today, it will make the next assignment requiring an expert interview that much harder and uncomfortable.

Another way to work through the fear and anxiety is to break down the assignment into the smallest steps and work through them one at a time. Sometimes it is just knowing how big the assignment is that overwhelms us. This will happen many times in your life, whether it is at work at school or even home projects. Write out a list of everything that needs to happen to complete the assignment in the smallest steps possible.

For example, for conducting an interview, you will most likely need to start with research, you'll need to collect contact information, and you'll have to make the first phone call. List down all of the steps and make them as small as possible. Then take another piece of paper and cover up everything except the first item.

Now, you can tell yourself that all you need to do is the uncovered item — that first item — to be closer to finishing the task. When the task is done, cross it out and move the paper down to the next item and repeat the process. Sometimes it really helps to keep the focus on the easiest, smallest steps rather than facing the weight of the entire assignment.

Another helpful practice is to keep everything in perspective. No matter what happens, the outcome is not what determines your worth. What is important is that you adhere to your values to the best of your ability. It is also usually helpful to communicate your struggles with your instructor as soon as possible. Sometimes they will give you reassurance, help you with additional resources, or on occasion, even offer you an extension.

Whenever you feel anxiety like this, try to acknowledge it as soon as possible. The earlier you take action, the more confident you will feel as time goes on. The worst thing you can do to yourself is procrastinate because it will only make the anxiety worse later — it will only make it that much more daunting of a task. The earlier you get to work, the better you will feel. Every time a situation like this occurs, it is an opportunity to practice overcoming these struggles. Every time you practice overcoming your fears and completing the task at hand — despite the outcome — the stronger your sense of self-efficacy will be. This will affect your confidence and future resilience, so next time you feel overwhelmed, take a deep breath and just try your best.

LEARN TO DEAL WITH "NO"

Certainly, no matter how proactive you are, there are times when you're not going to get the outcome you wanted and you're given a "no" in response to your request. As mentioned previously, getting rejected doesn't feel good and it might disappoint you or even make you angry, but learning how to deal with a "no" is critical to your future success.

The important thing to keep in mind is that while a "no" does mean "no," it's not necessarily personal. The person who isn't able to say "yes" isn't doing it to punish you or hurt you in any way. There are probably reasons behind their "no" that probably have nothing to do with you. Taking out this personal aspect of rejection can make it less hurtful because you know it's due to factors outside of your control.

The best way to find out why the person wasn't able to give you what you need is to directly ask them. For example, maybe your teacher really can't give you extra time on your project because it's the end of the term and they have to have all their grades in by a specific time. They have a deadline to meet, so you have to stick to your deadline as well.

Sometimes, there's a simple explanation for the rejection and once you understand why they're saying "no," it's easier for you to find an alternate solution.

Unfortunately, not everyone is going to give you a reason behind their decision. It could be an embarrassing reason to them (your parents can't give you a raise in your allowance because they're struggling financially themselves) or it could be that someone else made the decision but they have to deliver the bad news to you (you asked for Saturdays off at work, but the general manager requires your supervisor to hold you to your initial availability because they have a staffing shortage and no one to cover your shift).

People don't always owe you an explanation, but you have to remember that they probably aren't saying "no" because they don't like you or because they want you to fail. In all likelihood, the reasons are not personal to you at all.

Let's look at an example. You believe you would be more successful on an assigned project in your science class if you worked with a partner. Your teacher tells you "no," but doesn't give a reason for their answer. What could be possible reasons behind this decision?

- The project is designed to assess what each student knows about the topic. If there are two people working on the same project, the teacher is unable to assess each person's knowledge individually.
- The last time the teacher allowed partners, some people ended up doing all the work while others did nothing and both people got the same grade. In the interest of fairness, this project needs to be completed individually.
- The teacher is targeting all types of learning styles with their projects. Some will be completed in partners, some in groups, and some individually.
- The principal has told all teachers that they need to have fewer group projects and more individual assignments. Even though the teacher prefers to have students working in pairs or groups, they have to follow their principal's directions.
- There has been a recent uptick in conflicts between some students in class so the teacher decided to have students work alone on this project to diffuse those conflicts.

You can see that there are several reasons that might have led the teacher to make the decision they did, all of which had nothing to do with you personally. When you take a few moments to look at the decision objectively, you can begin to formulate your next move, whatever that may be. Chances are if you don't get what you need to follow your initial plan, you'll have to rethink your approach so you can get what you need to be successful.

Being proactive is usually rewarded, whether you get all of what you need or just some of it. Standing up for yourself and what you require to be successful is a necessary skill if you want to go as far as you can. Even if you get rejected and can't get what you think you need, being proactive allows you enough time to revise your initial plan so that you can find another, and perhaps better, way to the finish line.

COMPROMISE AND RESOLVE CONFLICTS

No matter how much you want to avoid conflict in your life, it's going to happen. You will need to know how to handle conflict and how to compromise with others to be successful in life, so the abilities to compromise and resolve conflicts are crucial success habits for teens.

UNDERSTAND COMPROMISES AND WIN-WIN SITUATIONS

The first thing you need to know is that you won't always win every conflict and you shouldn't even look at conflict as a win or lose proposition. In fact, you should view conflict as a negotiation where the ideal outcome is what is known as a win-win situation. This means that each party walks away from the conflict satisfied, having benefited from the negotiation. Many win-win situations involve some compromise, in which each person has to give up some of what they initially wanted.

While you don't always get everything you want in a compromise, you do get what you need and so does the other party. No one feels like they gave up too much and no one is unhappy with the results. Sometimes a successful compromise is difficult to achieve, especially if the people involved are stubborn and do not want to give up any of their demands. Stubbornness often leads to a stalemate, a lose-lose situation in which no one gets anything they want, or to a win-lose situation in which one of the parties eventually gives in to all of the other party's demands.

You might be tempted to think that a person who is always the winner in a win-lose scenario is the more successful person, but that's not usually the case. If someone is always forcing other people to give in to them to get what they want, they might not be viewed as successful; they could be seen instead as a bully who doesn't ever consider others' needs.

The more successful person is the one who considers everyone's goals and tries to find a solution that meets everyone's needs. This is often more difficult than using force to get everything you want, but it has a better outcome because your reputation will be intact and other people will feel good about working with you because they know you can compromise. This is why it's worth learning the skills necessary to facilitate win-win situations.

ASK FOR WHAT YOU WANT OR NEED

Asking for what you need is a big part of many success habits for teens, and for adults as well. Learning how to ask for what you need is a critical component of compromise and resolving conflicts. There are also some slight differences between asking for what you need to help you be successful and asking for what you want (or need) in a negotiation.

As mentioned in the Be Proactive section, sometimes asking for what you need turns into a negotiation, so if you prepare as if you're going to have to negotiate to get what you need, you'll be ready if that situation comes to pass. We discussed some of what you should prepare for in the earlier section, including having counterarguments ready to respond to the other party's objections, but there are some other preparations you'll want to make going into a negotiation.

Before you approach the other person or party to open negotiations, take the time to:

- Identify what you need or want - As with being proactive, you'll want to be direct when you begin negotiating with another person. Know what you want or need and ask for it. Aim high because in negotiations, you probably won't get everything you request, but you'll likely get some part of your request and you want to make sure that's satisfactory to you.

- Develop sound reasoning for what you need or want - When you ask for something, the person you're asking will want to know why you need or want it. Make sure you have solid reasons that support your position so the other person understands why it's important to you.

  For example, if you're asking your parents for a smartphone, you might argue that having one is necessary so that you can contact your parents in an emergency. Have several good reasons ready to share. The more evidence you can provide that you truly need what you're asking for, the harder it will be for the other person to argue against.

- Come to the table with counteroffers - As mentioned previously, in a negotiation, you will probably have to compromise to get what you want or need. This means giving up some of what you're hoping to get in return for the other party giving up some of what they want.

  If we take the example of asking for a smartphone, your parents might argue that they don't want you to have access to the Internet away from home. A counteroffer might be to get a basic cell phone that only allows texts and calls. It's not exactly what you want, but it's better than not having a cell phone at all. If that's not satisfactory to you, then you'll have to come up with a different counteroffer, such as only taking the phone with you when you're away from your parents.

Be sure to review the "How Do You Ask For What You Need?" section of Be Proactive to refresh yourself on other tips for approaching another person with a request. The timing and phrasing of your request are important no matter if there's going to be a negotiation or not, and it never hurts to practice before you initiate a conversation so you feel more confident and sure of yourself.

LISTEN

Active listening is a success habit for teens all of its own, which will be discussed in a later section, but it's a vital component of compromise and conflict resolution as well. If you're always interrupting the other person or thinking about what you're going to say while they're expressing their position in a negotiation, you're not going to understand where they're coming from and you're not going to be able to offer a solid counterargument to persuade them otherwise.

It can be easy to start thinking about how you're going to present a counterargument against something the other person said while they're still talking, but when you do that, you are no longer listening to what they have to say. Instead, you should have your potential counterarguments already thought out before you ever get to the negotiation, so you can listen carefully to what the other person says and not have to worry about formulating a counterargument then and there.

Of course, there will be times when the other person comes up with an argument that you don't have a counterargument for, but don't let that derail your approach to listening. You can always ask for a couple of minutes to gather your thoughts after the person is done speaking so you can formulate a response.

You can also say, "That's a good point. I'd like to consider it for a little while and return to this discussion later." This doesn't mean the other person "won." It just means they gave you something to think about. It might turn out you agree with them and don't need to negotiate anymore. Or, you'll still disagree with them and come up with a counterargument to rebut their point.

By demonstrating to the other person that you're carefully listening to them, they will usually mirror your actions and do the same for you. This is to your benefit because you need them to understand your reasoning behind your request and to take the time to consider it. When everyone involved in a negotiation is listening to each other, the chances for miscommunication and misunderstandings decrease significantly.

As mentioned previously, we'll go deeper into active listening in a future section because it's a habit you need to develop for all situations. This skill will help you in negotiations, meetings, classes, speaking with friends, and in many other areas of your life.

MANAGE YOUR EMOTIONS

This is a big one. Often, when we enter a negotiation, it's because we're not getting something we need or want and we're upset, angry, or anxious about that situation. But you can't let emotions rule your actions when you're in the middle of a negotiation. This is extremely challenging, especially when you haven't yet learned how to manage everything you might be feeling.

To begin with, you'll want to prepare yourself for any potential feelings that might arise during the negotiation process. By identifying and making a plan to manage these emotions ahead of time, you are more likely to be able to keep a clear head and a rational approach to your negotiation while it's happening.

Anxiety

You could be anxious about what the other person is going to say during your conversation; practicing how you're going to respond is the key to overcoming this obstacle. Studies have found that people who are anxious when they're negotiating make weaker offers and are more likely to accept less than they could get if they were more confident.

Try to have the negotiation in a familiar space because the more unfamiliar your surroundings, the more anxious you'll feel. If you can't hold the negotiation on your turf, ask for a meeting in a neutral location. This will ensure that both parties are on even ground when the process begins. This isn't always possible (for instance, if you're asking for an extension on an assignment, you'll probably have to be in your teacher's classroom), but if it is possible, being in an environment where you feel comfortable will lessen your anxiety.

When you practice what you're going to say during the negotiation, try to mimic the environment as much as possible. This is another way to expose you to the surroundings you might be in to reduce your feelings of anxiety. The more you practice for your negotiations, the more negotiations will feel comfortable in general, so eventually, you might not need to worry about the environment as much as you do at first.

Anger

Anger can rear its head when you don't feel like you're being heard or you're not getting anything you need out of the process. Often, we go into negotiations with the idea that they're competitions, but if we look at them as collaborations instead, we will have a more positive mindset before any negotiations even begin (more on this in a minute).

When you start to feel angry, keep in mind that the people involved are separate from the problem. Their position toward the subject at hand is not personal. Remember when we discussed that when people say "no" to your request, it has nothing to do with you? They have their own reasons for their decision.

The same is true for negotiations. People are not taking a position in opposition of yours because they don't like you or because they're trying to be difficult. They're taking the position they are because of specific reasons that they're probably going to share with you during the process.

For instance, your parents aren't opposed to giving you a smartphone because they're mean or trying to upset you. They might be worried about the impact of too much screen time on your brain or they could be trying to keep you safe from strangers on the Internet. Or, there could be a dozen other reasons behind their position. The point is that their position is not personal.

Likewise, your desire to have a smartphone is not personal toward your parents. Most likely, you don't want one just because it will make them worry less about you. You have your reasons for wanting or needing one and you will lay your position and argument out during the negotiations. Once you realize their opposition to you isn't personal, you can focus on solving the problem together.

If the other party is not budging on their stance at all, anger can become a problem during negotiations no matter how much you try to tamp it down. In this case, asking for a break is a perfectly acceptable strategy for managing your emotions. You want to protect the relationship you have with the other party and becoming very angry isn't a helpful way to care for that relationship.

Try to anticipate what will trigger your anger during a negotiation so you can prepare for that possibility. This will allow you to come up with a strategy to keep your anger in check or to signal that you need a break so you can get yourself back under control.

Keep in mind that a negotiation involves give and take, so if you're not budging on your position, maybe being the first one to give a little will diffuse the situation and allow you to get at least some of what you want. When two or more parties are being so stubborn that the negotiations are stalling and tensions are rising, nothing good will result from standing your ground.

Disappointment

As you have already learned, you probably aren't going to get everything you want out of a negotiation. After all, compromise is about both sides giving up a little bit to get most of what you want, but you still might feel disappointed if you don't come away from the process with something you can live with. It's okay to feel disappointed, but you should recognize that if you're disappointed, then you may have settled too quickly.

Studies have shown that people who are disappointed at their negotiation outcome believe they gave in too fast and that not enough back and forth occurred to ensure the other

66

side gave up as much as they did. The best way to make sure you're not disappointed with your results is to go into the negotiation knowing your absolute bottom line. What is the minimum you'll accept and be satisfied with the outcome? Now, you may not get that and if you don't, you may need to restart negotiations again at a later time, but if you get your minimum or more, you should be satisfied.

One way to stave off disappointment is to take your time during negotiations and don't agree to anything too quickly. Be deliberate when considering any offer and proceed slowly before committing to your part of the bargain. Think about all the consequences attached to what you're accepting to make sure you understand both sides' responsibilities to ensure you're going to be able to hold up your end. Sometimes, when we get what we want, we overlook what we are being required to do to get it. This can lead to disappointment after the fact.

Another great tactic to avoid disappointment is to spend a little time at the end making sure both sides are satisfied. You might say, "it looks like we've come to an agreement we can both live with, but let's take a few minutes to see if we can find anything else that can make the deal better for both of us." This gives each side a bit of time to really look at the proposed outcome to make sure they're truly satisfied. Make sure you're clear that you're not trying to renegotiate, but instead are just trying to make sure the results are good for everyone.

SET GROUND RULES

In addition to keeping people separate from the problem, setting ground rules can help you manage your emotions and ensure your relationship with the other party stays intact. Before any negotiation begins, all parties involved should discuss the ground rules for the process.

Setting ground rules should not prolong the negotiations in any way or become a point of negotiation themselves. If one party suggests a ground rule, most of the time, as long as it's reasonable, the ground rule should be adopted. The more that each party can contribute to deciding on the ground rules, the more comfortable everyone will be with the process. Of course, if there are really inappropriate suggestions, those can be discussed briefly, but in general, ground rules are meant to keep the process professional and collaborative.

In negotiations that might continue for several sessions, you probably want to write the ground rules down, but in a short negotiation, verbal ground rules are fine. Some common ground rules in negotiations include:

- Each person will get an opportunity to state their position or viewpoint
- No one will interrupt another person when it's their turn to talk
- If discussions get tense, anyone involved with the negotiations can request a break
- Everyone will be treated with respect, even if others disagree with them
- Participants agree to have a collaborative mindset rather than a competitive mindset
- Participants agree to be willing to compromise
- Participants will focus on the problem and not the people involved
- Participants will stay on topic
- Outcomes will be recorded

Of course, you can add any other ground rules you believe will be helpful in your negotiations, but you don't want your list to be too long. Again, this process isn't meant to take up a lot of time. It's just a framework for how you want the process to go so that emotions can stay in check for all parties.

REFRAME THE ISSUE AS A MUTUAL PROBLEM TO SOLVE

Rather than pitting one party against another in a negotiation, it's helpful to look at the issue as a mutual problem that needs to be solved. Even if you're asking for something that you want and the other person doesn't necessarily have to grant it to you, the issue can still be presented as a mutual problem that can be solved collaboratively.

For instance, if you want an extension on a project, you don't want the negotiation to be you versus the teacher. You want it to be you working with the teacher to come up with a mutually satisfactory solution. Instead of asking for an extension, then, you might say, "Is there a way I can get some extra time on this project that won't interfere with your grading timeline? I was thinking a one-week extension would work."

This approach shows that you acknowledge the inconvenience an extension would cause your teacher, but that you want to find a solution that works for both of you. Of course, the teacher still doesn't have to grant anything to you, but they will probably be more willing to consider your needs because you've framed it in a way that is collaborative rather than competitive.

A tip for reframing a negotiation is to use "we" statements instead of "I" or "you" statements. This tactic places all parties on the same side, working toward resolving the same problem. Even the most difficult negotiations become more positive if you approach them as a team instead of as opponents.

If the teacher says, "I am not going to give you a week longer than everyone else has had to work on this project," you could respond with, "What is an extension that we could both work with?" This shows that you're willing to work with the teacher to come up with a win-win solution. This automatically softens their stance by getting them to think about a way that they can still get what they need and give you some of what you need.

When you ask a question like the one above, you're acknowledging their view, but you're also allowing them space to come up with a counteroffer. For example, the teacher might then say, "I think I could give you an extra two days, but not a full week." You've already gotten a little bit of what you needed and the process is no longer about you versus them. It's about coming together to find a solution.

If there are more than two parties involved in a negotiation, make sure everyone engages in the solution. Otherwise, it might appear that two parties are ganging up on a third and that can trigger emotions that can derail the entire process.

If you see a party not participating, ask them what they think about a proposed solution or what they would do if they were in your shoes. These strategies will give them an opportunity to view the situation with a different lens and get them involved in the process.

PUT THE SOLUTION INTO ACTION

While the actual negotiation ends when a compromise is in place, there is still one more step to take to finalize the process. You and the other party have to put their agreed-upon responsibilities into action. If you agreed to get your first draft of a project submitted to the teacher on time, then make sure you do it. If the teacher promised to wait for three days after the due date to give you a final grade, then they need to hold up their end of the deal.

A compromise is only as solid as the people who agree to it, so you need to ensure you complete your responsibilities on time and in full. Don't come back to renegotiate the deal because that shows that you weren't committed to the process in the first place, and the other person will be less likely to want to negotiate with you in the future.

When a compromise has been reached, it's good to put the details of each party's responsibilities in writing. In fact, it should be one of your ground rules so that everyone knows what they need to do and when they need to do it. Every party involved in the negotiation should get a copy of the list of responsibilities. This way, you can set up a goal (see the

Set Goals section) to ensure you complete your responsibilities on time.

Remember that your reputation is on the line when you negotiate and agree to terms. If you don't keep your promises, not only will the other party not want to negotiate with you again, but they will also advise others not to negotiate with you either. It's never good to get what you want only to let down the other party so they don't get what they want. Holding up your end of the bargain is not only expected, but also a sign of maturity, so be sure to only agree to conditions that you absolutely intend and are able to keep.

PRACTICE WITH LOW-STAKES CONFLICTS

A recurring theme in this guide is practice and there's no exception here. The best way to get better at negotiating is to practice. You've probably already been negotiating throughout your entire life without even realizing it. Whenever you wanted a new toy, you likely had to give your parents something in return. Perhaps you promised to do extra chores or be quiet during church to get what you wanted, which your parents either accepted or rejected.

It's possible you even threw a temper tantrum when you didn't get what you wanted because your emotions got the best of you and that was one of the only ways you knew how to respond. If your parents gave in, it's probable that you threw other tantrums to get other things you wanted later. As you age, though, getting angry or upset isn't going to work anymore.

Now you know how to go into negotiations with a plan and how to keep your composure even if the other party initially says no, but you still need to practice managing your emotions in low-stakes situations. Low-stakes could mean bargaining with your siblings for different chores or for who gets to sit in the front seat of the car on a trip. Or it could mean negotiating with your parents over your curfew time, sleep-in time, or where you're going to go on vacation.

These negotiations are considered low-stakes because if you don't get what you want, they won't have a major impact on your life. Yes, you'd like to get what you ask for all the time, but starting small gives you the opportunity to refine your process and really learn how to rein in your emotions, set ground rules, and reframe the negotiation process from competitive to collaborative. Just remember to always keep your promises and fulfill your responsibilities to uphold your good reputation.

COMMUNICATE EFFECTIVELY

Whether you're an introvert or an extrovert, you will have to communicate throughout life to get what you need and to ensure you aren't misunderstood or misrepresented. Effective communication is a critical success habit for teens because the sooner you learn how to communicate effectively, the sooner you can engage with other people without getting frustrated and disappointed.

Communication comes in many forms: verbal, non-verbal, written, and visual. In fact, it's recommended that you always include two or more forms of communication when you're trying to get your point across to someone else. This helps ensure your message is heard and understood.

Once again, it's necessary to repeatedly practice all forms of communication to improve your skills and outcomes. You are probably going to be stronger in some areas and weaker in others, which is normal. You can work on strengthening those skills that don't come to you naturally, and also lean into the ones where you're already strong to make the most of your natural abilities in that area. Being a powerful communicator is a skill you can leverage for nearly any purpose.

ENGAGE IN REGULAR CONVERSATION

You can only get better at conversing with others by actually talking to other people. The more varied and numerous the people you talk to, the better!

Make time to talk to people from all walks of life to be exposed to different accents, dialects, vocabularies, and slang, all of which will enrich your own experiences and allow you to connect with others down the road. Seek out people of different ages and genders and with different backgrounds and interests. There is something to learn from everyone; not only will your communication skills improve over time, but you can make new friends and learn any number of things you never knew before through these conversations.

It can be very intimidating to start a conversation with someone you don't know, especially if you're not used to speaking with strangers. After all, your parents have probably long cautioned you not to talk to strangers at all. Certainly, if you don't feel comfortable approaching someone to talk, you shouldn't do it. But as you get older, there will be safe opportunities to talk to people you don't know in controlled environments (during a college tour or at your part-time job, for example).

When you just don't know how to start a conversation with someone you don't know, try one of these tactics:

- Ask for an opinion. People love to give their views on just about anything. If you're at school, ask the person seated at the desk next to you if they like the subject of the class. If you're at an event, ask the person sitting next to you what they think of the decorations. You probably don't want to ask them anything controversial, so stick to safe subjects when you're just trying to meet someone.

- Ask for advice or recommendations. As with their opinions, people like to feel like an expert on things, even things as small as which meal to try at a restaurant. This is a great question to ask the person in line behind you before you order. You can also comment on something a person is wearing and ask them where they got it from.

- comment on the environment. You can find something to comment on no matter where you are. If you're in a room that's overly stuffy, you can comment on the heat. If you're in an elevator, you can comment on the choice of music or how long it takes to get to your floor. The point is to invite the other person to comment as well, perhaps sparking a longer conversation.

- Ask simple open-ended questions. You don't want to ask overly difficult questions because that represents a risk for the other person, who may not know the answers. Instead, ask simple open-ended questions so that the person has to respond with more than "yes" or "no," but won't put them on the spot. For instance, asking the person manning the rec center check-in desk when the best time to work out is will give them a chance to show off their expertise and give advice at the same time. If you say, "Is 9:00 a.m. a good time to work out?" instead, you're indicating you just want a "yes" or "no" answer and don't want to chat.

- Ask about hobbies or interests. People enjoy talking about themselves, so if you know a little bit about someone or can make a guess about what they like doing based on what you're doing together, asking about their hobbies or interests can really get someone talking. You might observe someone playing soccer in the park and then have a chance to talk to them at the drinking fountain. You might ask if they're on a team or comment on their skill level.

WRITE WITH INTENTION

You need to know how to communicate in writing whether your audience is formal or casual.

Throughout school, you have learned and will continue to learn how to write for specific audiences, usually in the form of essays. Some classes might teach business writing, which will often cover formal email writing as well. You will probably have to take responsibility for learning how to communicate through text and other messaging systems.

You might say that you've been texting all your life and know how to get your point across, but are you going to text the same way to everyone? What if your future boss texts you for an update on a project you're leading and you respond with "I got u bro"? This is not only inappropriate for communication with a boss, but it's also not very clear what you mean with your brief statement.

In a case like this, your boss might assume from those words that everything's taken care of when what you meant was you're behind schedule but you'll have it done as soon as possible. Your boss can't possibly understand what you mean by those four words and they set the stage for a major miscommunication issue.

Understanding how to write for all types of audiences is critical to your success as a communicator. Fortunately, you can take steps to immediately improve your written communication skills. Here's how.

- Think about purpose. Why are you writing to this person? What do you want them to understand when they read your message? In the example above, do you want your boss to know that you have everything under control and that the project is progressing on schedule? Or do you need to let them know that you've run into a roadblock and what you need to handle that challenge? "I got u bro" doesn't communicate any of that, so you wouldn't be fulfilling the purpose of your response.

- Put yourself in your audience's shoes. Are they going to understand certain abbreviations? Should you even use abbreviations with this person? Do they already have background knowledge on what you're writing about? Before you hit send or submit your writing, read through what you've written as if you're the audience so you can see where a misunderstanding might occur.

- Be concise. There's no reason to use fancy words or long paragraphs if a sentence or two with simple words will suffice. Get to the point of your message quickly and consider whether the person you're writing to will understand technical jargon or if you need to use non-technical language. In most cases, you won't be writing for a grade, so you just need to make sure your message is understood. Use as many words as you need to ensure there is no misunderstanding, but don't overdo it just to fill space.

- Proofread. Especially when your audience is formal, take time to proofread your text, email, or message before you send it. While some applications allow you to edit your writing after you send it, most do not. You are stuck with what you sent. Typos and spelling errors not only reflect poorly on you, but can also create uncertainty about what you're trying to say.

- Edit. A good habit to get into is to always edit your writing before you send it. Read the message out loud to ensure it makes sense. Remove unnecessary words or sentences that are getting in the way of conciseness. Make sure there is no inferred tone that could indicate that you're angry or upset with the reader. Remember that you can't always get a response back so you'll have to deal with any consequences that come from unedited writing.

- Read and write a lot. Yes, we're going to talk about practice again. You can improve your own writing by reading others' written works and by practicing writing various types of documents. Take notes in meetings and classes that can help you compose messages later. Sometimes, you'll find that your notes weren't very good and that you need to improve that part of your writing practice so you can make your final drafts better. If you have to write a specific type of document you've never written before, look for examples online and emulate their structure, tone, and style.

- Be intentional. These days, it's easy to shoot off a text or an email without a second thought, but continuously doing that will cause you to develop bad writing habits. Instead, keep in mind that everything you write is usually a permanent record (even if it's deleted, it can probably be recovered) and approach all messages with intention. Always consider your audience, their background, the consequences of sending a poorly composed message, and your own reputation before you ever hit the send button.

USE APPROPRIATE AND RESPECTFUL VOCABULARY

Verbal and written communication have one thing in common: vocabulary. The more words you know, the better you will be able to communicate your feelings, needs, and wants. Using incorrect or inappropriate words can cause misunderstandings and impact your audience's attitude toward you. Of course, the vocabulary you use will depend on your audience and circumstances, but learning to know when to use specific words is a skill that will always come in handy.

Vocabulary is tightly linked to "saying what you mean" in both verbal and written communication. Even though some words can have a similar meaning, sometimes their connotation is very different and may change the entire interpretation of what you're trying to say.

For instance, a thesaurus will tell you that the word "stench" is a synonym for "odor," which is technically correct. However, "stench" has a negative connotation, whereas "odor" can be either positive or negative. If you say to someone that their perfume has a pleasant stench, they aren't going to take that as a compliment, but saying their perfume has a pleasant odor is much more positive. However, an even better sentence would be "your perfume has a pleasant aroma."

Knowing the difference between the subtle meanings of "odor," "stench," and "aroma" allows you to compliment

86

someone instead of insulting them. Even if you didn't mean to insult them, your inappropriate use of a vocabulary word did it for you. It might be difficult to recover from this type of miscommunication.

In addition to using appropriate vocabulary for your audience and situation, you also want to use respectful vocabulary with everyone. Slurs, slang, and curse words are usually not respectful, especially in formal settings. But, even if you're just speaking to your friends, there are some words you should never use if you want to remain respectful. While we won't go into detail here, refraining from using disrespectful vocabulary is vital to your reputation.

Words that Stop Communication

Along with knowing which words to use when, you should also be aware of words that tend to stop communication. Words are powerful, and whether your audience realizes it or not, certain words stop the communication process cold. If you're trying to keep the lines of communication with you open, avoid these words:

- But - There's a saying that says when you use the word "but," it means forget everything you said before it and everything after it is what you really mean. Using "but" gives the audience mixed messages and also signals to them that you're placating them by saying things you don't really mean before saying what you really do mean.

For instance, instead of saying, "I really like your approach, but what if we tried this one instead?" try saying "I really like your approach and maybe we can try this one as well." The change is subtle, but conveys authenticity and honesty, both of which are important in communication.

- Assume - When you use the word "assume," your listener gets the message that you didn't really listen to them because you're assuming their position or views rather than actually stating it.
- Actually - This word is often used before you correct someone, and no one likes to be corrected, especially in public. Of course, people make mistakes, but using "actually" before you correct them feels a lot like rubbing it in.
- Honestly - Hopefully, you're always being honest when you're communicating, otherwise, what's the

point? Putting "honestly" at the beginning of what you're going to say actually says the opposite. People frequently say "honestly" before they say something dishonest. Even if you don't intend it this way, it has that effect on the audience, so just leave it off.

- No offense - This phrase is used when people want to say something offensive and get away with it. It's a passive-aggressive way of saying something rude and your audience will see it as rude anyway.

- Nope - This word is both dismissive and disrespectful. There are dozens of ways to say no without closing off communications. "Nope" isn't one of them. This shuts everything down immediately and the other party will hesitate communicating with you in the future.

Actively Listen

We told you earlier that we'd get back to the subject of listening, since it's a skill that will serve you well in multiple parts of your life. Active listening is a critical part of communication because communication goes both ways. You have to get your message across, but you also need to hear the messages other people are sending.

Active listening encourages honesty and openness. It also sets the standard for how you want others to treat you when you're speaking. If you're demonstrating active listening skills, others will follow your lead. Of course, not everyone is good at this skill, so it might take some time for everyone to be on board.

When you're listening to someone who is speaking, make sure to indicate you are actively listening by:

- Giving the speaker your full attention - Don't stare out a window or use your phone while someone is talking. Even if you're hearing the words they're saying, you're not really listening to them. Face the speaker and keep your gadgets in your purse or pocket.

- Being aware of your non-verbal communication - We can say a lot without saying anything at all. Our non-verbal communication and body language tell the speaker you're really listening to them or that you're not listening at all. Be very conscious of your facial expressions, which can give thoughts away in a flash. Smile and nod at the speaker to encourage them to continue and to indicate you're really hearing what they say.

Eye contact and tracking the speaker when they move are two other non-verbal cues that show you're listening. You don't have to stare them down, but when they look at you and make eye contact, it's okay to hold it for a second or two. Make sure you're a comfortable distance away from the speaker so that you're not invading their space. This can make someone very uncomfortable and make them rush through their message.

- Avoiding interrupting - As mentioned before in the Compromise and Resolve Conflicts section, interrupting a speaker is a sign of disrespect. It signals to them that what you have to say is more important than what they have to say. If you think of something you want to say during their turn, write a brief note to yourself to remind you to mention it when it's your turn. You should also wait a few seconds after someone finishes a sentence before jumping in to make sure they're truly finished.

- Asking questions - At appropriate times (during natural pauses, when the speaker asks for questions, after they're finished talking, etc.), ask relevant questions that show you have been paying attention to them and that you are interested in knowing more about or clarifying their position or topic. Don't ask questions that have already been answered, though, or that will demonstrate that you weren't really listening.

Good questions are open-ended, allowing the speaker to provide extra information to clarify their statements. "Yes" or "no" questions don't offer the opportunity for clarification, which should be the point of any questions during or immediately after a speech.

- Summarizing what was said - When the speaker is finished with their turn, it's a good practice to summarize what they said so the speaker can correct any misconceptions and can tell that you truly listened to their words. You don't have to go into much depth, just say, "what I heard you say is..." or "if I understand correctly, you said.." and provide a really quick summary. This way, you can demonstrate your listening skills and ensure both parties are communicating clearly.

- Taking turns - This tip goes along with not interrupting, but it's important enough to reiterate. When it's the other person's turn to talk, it's your turn to listen. When it's your turn to talk, that's when you can refute what was said, bring up your own points, and offer examples and evidence. You can even use a "talking stick" (whoever has the stick is the one talking and everyone else is listening) or a timer to ensure everyone gets a chance to say their piece without anyone interrupting. This is a good practice in a larger group.

Active listening is one of the hardest habits to develop because we are programmed to be thinking about what we want to say when the other person is talking. We can get stuck on one point that the speaker made and stop listening to everything else while we formulate a response. The temptation to do this is difficult to curb, but it's the key to really hearing what another person says.

We are a distracted society and active listening is a skill that is more difficult to develop as an adult than in childhood. By starting now, you can practice the finer points of active listening so that by the time you become an adult, you'll be a step ahead of everyone else.

EXERCISE

Developing the habit of exercise when you're young can set yourself up for a lifetime of movement, making yourself healthier and happier. Exercise doesn't only improve your body; it also improves your mental state of mind and overall wellbeing.

BENEFITS OF EXERCISE

You are probably already aware of some of the benefits of exercise, but there are so many that you might not know all of them. Society's focus is on the benefit of weight control because there is a current obesity epidemic that needs to be reversed. Maintaining a healthy weight is important for long-term health. But there are also many other reasons to develop an exercise habit.

CARDIOVASCULAR HEALTH

Most of us already know that exercise is good for the heart and cardiovascular system. Exercise increases the muscles' ability to draw oxygen from your blood, which means your heart doesn't have to work as hard to oxygenate your body. This allows the heart to function at top condition for a longer time.

Moreover, exercise causes your heart rate to slow down, thereby reducing blood pressure and it reduces stress hormones, which can place an extra burden on your heart. To get the most of these heart-healthy benefits, you'll want to participate in a combination of aerobic (running, biking, swimming, walking) and resistance training (weightlifting).

BONE AND MUSCLE STRENGTH

Exercise strengthens muscles by breaking down the muscles, allowing them to rebuild themselves over time so that they are thicker and stronger. In addition, exercise strengthens your bones. Similar to muscles, bones are living tissues, so they will change over time in response to the amount of force that's placed upon them.

As you exercise and exert pressure on your bones, your body responds by growing more bone and making them denser. This is especially important as you age and your body naturally loses bone density, making them more fragile and prone to fractures. The sooner you can begin to build up your muscles and bones, the less you'll have to worry about losing muscle and bone density when you're older.

ANXIETY AND DEPRESSION RELIEF

Most people experience feelings of anxiety or depressed mood at some times, and these can be difficult to handle. Regular exercise triggers the release of feel-good endorphins from your brain, lifting your mood and reducing stress levels not only while you're exercising, but also afterwards.

In fact, the positive effects of exercise on mood can last for hours, if not days, and studies have shown that stress affects regular exercisers less than it does those who don't exercise on a regular basis. So, you're not only distracting yourself from stressors in your life while you exercise, but you're also building a reservoir of stress-fighting hormones that you can use during the times when you feel anxious or depressed.

BETTER SLEEP

While experts don't fully understand how exercise makes you sleep better, they have some theories. One is simply that exercise tires you out, making you ready for a good night's sleep each night. Another idea is that exercise raises your core body temperature, which is a signal for you to be awake, but when that core temperature drops a couple of hours later, that tells your body it's time to sleep.

What we do know for sure is that exercise increases the amount of deep sleep you get, which is the most rejuvenating part of the sleep cycle. This might be related to the effects exercise has on the heart by slowing the heart rate, but it also might be connected to the mental health benefits of exercise. When you're not stressed and your mood is stable, you're in the right state to fall asleep and stay asleep.

SOCIAL OPPORTUNITIES

Exercising regularly also gives you social opportunities that you might not otherwise have. Whether you run through a park every day or go to the gym, you're bound to meet some of the same people on a regular basis. It offers the perfect chance to strike up conversation with these fellow exercisers and get to know them better. If you're looking for an opportunity to practice your conversation skills, exercising with other people provides an ideal opening.

GETTING INTO
THE EXERCISE HABIT

As with any habit, exercising regularly is something you'll have to work to develop and it won't work unless you're committed to it. Setting goals (see the Set Goals section) will help you accomplish smaller steps until you reach your ultimate exercise goals. This process will be much easier and more enjoyable if you choose an activity you really like. If you hate running and you decide that you want to start running because it's what your friends do, you aren't going to stick with it, and you don't need to try to stick with something that doesn't feel right for your body.

If you're already part of a sports team, you're on your way to establishing a habit because you'll have set practice and game days that can count toward your exercise goals. If you don't participate in sports yet and you want to, research the sports that are available in your area and join one that interests you. Check your school's offerings as well as those through recreation centers and gyms. You can even ask your friends if you can join their teams or leagues as well.

There are also plenty of non-sport activities that will give you the exercise you need. Swimming is an excellent activity that is easy on your joints while at the same time strengthening your muscles and increasing your cardiovascular health. Other activities you can do on your own that can increase your activity level include walking, bowling, golf, running/jogging, jumping rope, lifting weights, bike riding, rollerblading, skateboarding, and more.

If you're having trouble finding an activity that you enjoy, think about what you used to do when you were younger. Many kids love to ride bikes and if you enjoyed that at one time, the odds are you'll enjoy it now. You might need some equipment to get you started, but once you have it, you'll probably develop an exercise habit fairly quickly.

After discovering the exercise or exercises you want to do regularly, it's time to create a schedule. When are you going to participate in your activities? Some experts suggest that exercising the first thing in the morning offers more benefits than doing it later in the day.

When you exercise in the morning, your body is already burning excess calories before you start your day and will continue burning those calories throughout the day. By waiting until the afternoon or evening to work out, your body isn't in calorie-burning mode for nearly as long. However, most experts will tell you that it doesn't actually matter much when you work out as long as you do it, so choose the schedule that works best for you.

By scheduling your exercise sessions into your day, you're making it a priority (see the Prioritize section). It's a task that you can check off your list when it's done and feel like you accomplished at least one of your daily goals. Of course, there may be other priorities or even higher priorities on your list from day to day, but keeping exercise on your list is important, if not urgent.

If you're having trouble meeting your exercise goal, consider asking a friend to join you. An accountability buddy can help you reach goals that you are struggling to achieve. Since one of the benefits of exercise is social opportunities, why not start off by taking that to heart and finding other people who are looking to make exercise a habit themselves? It might just be the push you — and they — need to get started.

Keep in mind that as you're developing an exercise habit, you're doing something good for your body and mind. Even if you're not worried about your health right now, creating an exercise habit is one that will pay off physically and mentally for years to come.

HAVE HOBBIES

Have you ever heard the saying that all work and no play makes Jack a dull boy? What this means is that if you don't take time to have some fun and spend all your days working, you might not feel very fulfilled by your life. Make sure you find a balance that works for you between time spent on responsibilities and working, and time dedicated to relaxation and fun.

To this end, make a habit of having and participating in hobbies. It doesn't really matter what your hobbies are as long as you enjoy them and they aren't harming anyone else. Often, people start their hobbies when they're very young and show an interest in an activity that they're encouraged to pursue. But sometimes, it takes a bit of effort to find something you truly enjoy doing as a hobby. Once you do, though, you're setting yourself up for lifelong benefits.

BENEFITS OF HOBBIES

Of course, the main benefit of a hobby is that it allows you to relax and participate in something that releases those endorphins we discussed in the Exercise section. When those hormones hit your brain, it wants more of them. Your brain then relates that feeling with the activity you were doing when it happened, thereby encouraging you to do it again.

In this way, hobbies can act like exercise for the brain, even if you're not physically exerting yourself during the activity. The endorphins that are released during the activity improve your mood, decrease your stress levels, and boost your feelings of self-worth, all of which are important for your mental health. But there are many other benefits to having hobbies than just making yourself feel good.

DISCOVER PASSIONS THAT COULD LEAD TO A CAREER

You've probably heard the phrase that if you love your job, you never work a day in your life. Well, that's a little simplistic, but it's mostly true. If you can get a career in something you have a passion for, it makes it a lot easier to get up and go to work every day. Hobbies can tell you what you're interested in and what you're good at, both of which can help you find a career that takes advantage of your enjoyment and skills.

For instance, if your hobby is gardening, you might consider a career in horticulture or landscaping. You could become a groundskeeper, a forester, a florist, a botanist, or any number of other careers that involve plants. Hobbies reveal our inner passions and sometimes can lead us to a job that is both fulfilling and meaningful.

BUILD SELF ESTEEM

As you dedicate time and energy to your hobbies, you may find that you develop strong skills related to that hobby, and that you become really good at it. It's human nature to enjoy things that we do well, and when we excel at something, it builds our self-esteem, which can increase our belief that we can be successful not only with this hobby, but with related hobbies as well.

Being a teenager can be challenging for a variety of reasons, and it's important that you participate in activities that consistently boost the way you feel about yourself. Many teens find this component of hobbies in sports, but there are multitudes of other hobbies that increase self-esteem. When those flowers you planted in spring bloom in summer, you feel accomplished. When you meet the objective in your video game, you feel proud. You can shut down any negative self-talk that you might have during other times of your day and just focus on your success.

Regulate Emotions

Remember when we discussed regulating emotions in the Compromise and Resolve Conflicts section? Having hobbies can help teach you this challenging skill. Of course, it doesn't mean that you won't get angry, anxious, or disappointed when you're in the middle of a heated negotiation, but it does mean that you won't enter into the negotiation as stressed or worried as you otherwise might.

This is because hobbies, as previously mentioned, reduce stress and promote a sense of well-being. When you're naturally calmer going into stressful situations, you're less likely to let your emotions get out of control. Taking time to participate in your hobbies will give you more emotional bandwidth to deal with the difficulties that will inevitably come your way.

HANDLE ADVERSITY

Things aren't always going to be smooth sailing, even when you're participating in a hobby you enjoy. But adversity is often more easily overcome when you're facing a challenge that prevents you from doing the things you love. You want to move past the roadblocks quickly so you can continue to pursue your passions.

What you may not realize, though, is that the strategies you learn when dealing with these challenges will greatly benefit you when you face difficult circumstances in other areas of your life. You're building resilience when you push through challenges so that you can keep doing what you love, and that resilience will help you make your way through other adverse situations as well.

TRY DIFFERENT HOBBIES

Even if you think you've found the perfect hobby for you and you have no interest in others, it is still a good idea to give them a try. The main reason for this is that you might discover something you enjoy as much or even more than the one you currently have. Even if you find that you don't enjoy a new activity as much, that allows you to return to your original hobby with a renewed confidence that it's the right thing for you.

Other reasons to try other different hobbies include developing new skills, meeting new people, and gaining new knowledge. There are so many activities available to you these days that you could try a new one every day and never run out of new experiences, but you don't have to go that far. Trying a couple of new hobbies every now and then is all it takes to broaden your life.

CLUBS

There are clubs for everything under the sun, from photography to books and rock climbing to chess. No matter what your interest is, there is likely a club that focuses on that interest. Your high school likely has numerous clubs that are open to students and this is a great place to start looking for one that meets your needs. School clubs are often chosen based on student interest, so if you want to start a club, all you need is a few friends who want to participate and a teacher willing to sponsor it.

Clubs can also be found at recreation centers, community centers, and online (but be careful of meeting strangers without your parents' approval, even virtually). Whether you have an interest in mind or you're looking to spark your interest by seeing what's available, you can usually browse a club catalog for an organization on that organization's website.

CLASSES AND WORKSHOPS

Teenagers might not want to add more classes to their already heavy workload, but taking classes in something you're interested in pursuing as a hobby is an excellent way to experience that hobby and determine if it's a good match. Some of these classes may be offered as electives at your high school (e.g., drama, band, newspaper, yearbook) and others can often be found for relatively low cost through community and recreation centers.

Often, hobby classes are offered through museums, community colleges, businesses (specifically those that deal in the arts), and government facilities, but these might cost more than those found at community and recreation centers. It doesn't hurt to look at their class catalogs to at least get an idea of something you might enjoy doing. If you don't find one you can afford, you can always save up to take the class you found or keep looking for a less expensive version.

Workshops are very similar to classes, but often have a hands-on component that classes may lack. Frequently, workshops are a component of classes so that you can put what you learn in class into practice at the workshop. You'll still have the benefit of a teacher present while you participate in the workshop, but you'll actually be doing the activity yourself.

SCHOOL EVENTS

There will never be another time in your life when you have access to so many events for little to no fee. The more school events you participate in, the more exposure you'll get to potential hobbies. For instance, if you participate in decorating your class float for the Homecoming Parade, you could discover a hidden talent for sculpting styrofoam or painting. It may sound far-fetched, but you just never know what skills you could acquire when you're participating in school events.

This is the time in your life when you have the freedom to explore as many hobbies as you want. Take advantage of the events your school puts on to not only create meaningful memories and meet other students from all walks of life, but also to explore hobbies that are new to you. The opportunities you have now won't always be available, so prioritize school events and volunteer for various roles to gain a wide range of experience.

PRACTICE SELF-CARE

Until just recently, this guide would have ended with the Have Hobbies section, but people are now realizing that there's another success habit that is just as important as the others discussed here. Self-care is about making yourself a priority at times to ensure you have the right balance of certain necessities to live a healthy life — mind, body, and soul.

BENEFITS OF SELF-CARE

Having hobbies and making time to participate in them is definitely a part of self-care, but it's not the only part, which is why this section is included. To be successful for the long term, it's important that you prioritize yourself and your needs so that you can function at your optimal level. When you don't put yourself first at times, your physical and mental health will suffer, which in turn, can make you less successful.

112

REDUCED ANXIETY, DEPRESSION AND STRESS SYMPTOMS

When you take the time to practice self-care, you're allowing your body and mind to relax and release the stress from other parts of your life. School, work, family obligations, social obligations, and other outside influences can drain your energy tanks. When you have nothing left to give, everything seems like a stressor and adds to your anxiety levels.

Stress is also linked closely with depression, as long-term stress knocks our psyche out of balance and can cause us to sink into a hole that can be challenging to escape. When we make time to participate in healthy activities that trigger the release of endorphins in our brain, we are better able to manage stress because we know it's not going to be there all the time. As a result, we can also use self-care to bring ourselves out of depression.

IMPROVED CONCENTRATION

The world is a noisy place and it can be hard to pay attention to any one thing for long if we're constantly bombarded by demands from others. Practicing self-care looks a lot of different ways for every person. If you are an introvert, spending quiet time by yourself or with trusted family and friends to escape the noise may allow you to focus on things that really matter to you. Whereas if you are an extrovert, you may need a night out socializing to feel recharged and grounded.

Not only are you better able to focus while you're practicing self-care, but when you return to the busy outside world, you can concentrate better there too. This is because you've refreshed your mind and centered yourself. You've refilled your energy tanks and now you can tackle necessary tasks with renewed vigor.

REDUCED FRUSTATION

Frustration is closely connected to stress because when we feel like we're under pressure to get something done or to solve a problem, we reach our frustration tolerance level more quickly than when we can figure something out at our own pace. This is why if we can step away from a situation where we're getting frustrated for a few minutes, we can usually tamp down our frustration and keep going.

But when our frustration tolerance level is low, not even stepping away for a few minutes will help. At that point, we aren't getting our self-care needs met and it's manifesting as quick frustration. We need to do something that we're good at so that our frustration tolerance level will return to normal. Or maybe we need to get the proper amount of sleep so that tiredness isn't impacting our temperament.

INCREASED ENERGY

Every day, we're confronted with tasks and people who drain a little bit of our energy. Sometimes, they drain a lot of it. The only way to refill your energy tanks is to spend time doing things that energize you. This could mean participating in your hobbies, going out to lunch with a friend, visiting family members, sleeping, going to church, exercising, or just spending time alone.

The key to keeping your energy levels balanced is to practice these self-care activities a little every day. Otherwise, your tanks will get completely depleted and you won't have energy to do anything. If you practice self-care enough, you'll start to recognize when your energy levels are low and you'll automatically prioritize self-care to bring them back up.

BOOSTED IMMUNE SYSTEM

A tired, stressed, poorly fed body is not a healthy one. It is a body that has a lowered immune system that is open to all sorts of illnesses. When we get enough sleep, eat properly, exercise, and take care of our mental health, we're boosting our immune system to defend the body against microscopic intruders that can make us sick.

This isn't to say that if you practice self-care strategies you'll never get sick again, but your body will be refreshed enough to better fight off illnesses that would otherwise force you to take a break. Often, we don't recognize that we're making ourselves more susceptible to illness when we're not taking care of ourselves until our body simply won't function properly anymore. This can be avoided by engaging in self-care activities on a regular basis.

PROPER SLEEP

As a teenager, you might love staying up all night and feel like you're able to function well even when you haven't gotten much sleep, but this isn't true. Even if you believe you're functioning at your fullest with very little sleep, your body is actually slowly deteriorating. Teens that don't get enough sleep are at higher risk for all sorts of health problems in the future, including diabetes, obesity, mental health issues, and issues with behavior and attention.

According to the American Academy of Sleep Medicine, teenagers between the ages of 13 and 18 should get between eight and ten hours of sleep every 24 hours. Currently, 72.2% of high school students report getting less than eight hours of sleep every night, which means nearly three-quarters of teenagers are not functioning at their best on a daily basis. It may be true that some people need more sleep than others, but those who consistently get an inadequate amount of sleep each night will eventually be faced with the health consequences of that behavior.

While it may feel challenging when your schedule is busy, prioritizing sleep is important and needs to be a part of your regular self-care habit.

The benefits of proper sleep include:

- More energy
- Improved concentration
- Improved mood
- Increased productivity
- Weight control
- Boosted immune system

As you can see, the benefits of getting enough sleep closely align with the benefits of self-care overall. This is not a coincidence. Making sure you sleep enough is one of the best things you can do for your body and mind.

PROPER NUTRITION

Learning how to feed your body is a vital part of self-care because the right approach to nutrition can give you energy and wellbeing, while missing out on proper nutrition can drain your energy and have a host of other negative consequences. The earlier you can make a habit of getting proper nutrition, the better off your body will be as you get older.

John Muir Health recommends teenagers eat a balanced diet that is rich in fruits, vegetables, whole grains, low- or non-fat dairy, eggs, fish, beans, nuts, and lean meats. The amount you should eat depends on your lifestyle and weight.

The benefits of eating a proper diet and getting the nutrition your body requires include

- Improved health
- Weight control
- Improved mood
- Disease and illness prevention
- Increased energy
- Strong bones, teeth, and brain

Again, many benefits of getting proper nutrition align with the overall benefits of self-care. Your body can't function at its best when you're feeding it candy and chips every day. Of course, you can always enjoy a treat, but the key, as with most other things in life, is balance.

SPIRITUALITY

The spiritual component of self-care is open to many definitions and interpretations. Some people will find their spiritual connection in a church, synagogue, or mosque. Others will find it in nature or at a meditation retreat. The concept of spirituality is discovering your personal connection with something bigger than yourself, whatever that may look like for you.

However you practice spirituality, it's important to include it as a regular part of your self-care routine. It gives you time to quiet your mind, get in touch with your emotions, clarify your personal goals, and diminish feelings of loneliness and isolation.

We spend a lot of time on building relationships with others, and many of the success habits in this guide are tips for managing those relationships, but spirituality is often about taking the time to get to know yourself. Whether you do this in a formal religious setting or an informal environment, by yourself or with others, you are increasing your sense of well-being and interconnectedness with the world.

The benefits of regularly practicing spirituality include:

- Connection with self and others
- Better decisions (thanks to improved clarity)
- Improved self-esteem
- Positive relationships
- Reduced anxiety and stress

It can be helpful to spend time learning about various spiritual activities and environments to find the one that resonates with you. Remember, this is about self-care, so while others can give their opinions on what spirituality means to them, what you're seeking is what spirituality looks like for you.

CONCLUSION

By developing the habits discussed in this guide now, you're setting yourself up for a lifetime of success. Of course, you'll experience failures, too, but as we mentioned in the Proactivity section, the key to dealing with failure is to turn it into a learning opportunity. If you reframe your failures as education, you can never really fail.

Keep in mind that change happens slowly, so if you don't already have some of these habits, don't expect to acquire them all overnight. In fact, tackling them one at a time is a perfect way to ensure you build lasting habits instead of fleeting preoccupations. Start by setting goals, which is going to help you as you develop the other habits in this guide.

You also don't have to establish these habits on your own. There are plenty of supportive people in your life who can help you meet your goals. Reach out to your parents, teachers, coaches, religious leaders, and friends to guide you along your journey toward success. Who knows? They might even join you and work on developing these habits themselves!

Made in United States
Orlando, FL
26 July 2023

35481848R00072